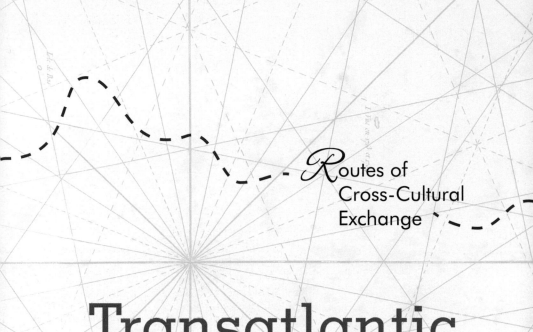

Routes of Cross-Cultural Exchange

Transatlantic Slave Networks

Pamela D. Toler

Cavendish Square

New York

Published in 2018 by Cavendish Square Publishing, LLC
243 5th Avenue, Suite 136, New York, NY 10016

Copyright © 2018 by Cavendish Square Publishing, LLC

First Edition

Library of Congress Cataloging-in-Publication Data

Names: Toler, Pamela D.
Title: Transatlantic slave networks / Pamela D. Toler.
Description: New York : Cavendish Square, 2018. | Series: Routes of cross-cultural exchange | Includes index.
Identifiers: ISBN 9781502626967 (library bound) | ISBN 9781502626905 (ebook)
Subjects: LCSH: Slave trade--History--Juvenile literature. |Slave trade--United States--History--Juvenile literature. |Slave trade--Africa--History--Juvenile literature.
Classification: LCC HT871.T65 2018 | DDC 382.4409--dc23

Editorial Director: David McNamara
Editor: Caitlyn Miller
Copy Editor: Alex Tessman
Associate Art Director: Amy Greenan
Designer: Jessica Nevins
Production Coordinator: Karol Szymczuk
Photo Research: J8 Media

Printed in the United States of America

Table of Contents

Three Hundred Years of Greed and Grief

Over the course of three hundred years, from the sixteenth century through the mid-nineteenth century, slave-trading ships from Europe and North America made more than 54,000 voyages along the triangular route of the transatlantic trade route. These ships carried some thirteen million Africans to be sold into slavery.

The Atlantic slave trade was one of the great crimes against humanity. But unlike the Armenian Genocide of 1915 or the Holocaust of World War II, the slave trade was not driven by fear and hatred. The only motive behind the capture, enslavement, and forced immigration of millions of people from the **sub-Saharan** region of Africa to the Americas was greed. European merchants wanted markets for their goods and inexpensive raw materials with which to make those goods. African slavers wanted goods offered by European traders— and the political and social power those goods represented. Colonial settlers wanted cheap labor to work in the mines and plantations of Americas,

Conditions on slave ships were horrific. African captives were packed into small spaces without privacy or room to move.

so they could export precious metals and agricultural products back to Europe.

In this book, we will look at how the transatlantic slave trade began and how it worked. We will also see how it linked Europe, Africa, Asia, and the Americas together into the first truly global economy.

We begin with an international slave trade that existed in Africa for centuries before European explorers and traders arrived on the West African coast in the fifteenth century. Arab merchants from North Africa traveled across the Sahara in **camel caravans** to trade for gold and slaves.

For several centuries, North African merchants were middlemen between sub-Saharan Africa and the rest of the Islamic and Mediterranean worlds. They had effective **monopolies** on both African gold and African slaves. In the fifteenth century that changed, when Prince Henry of Portugal organized expeditions to explore the West African coast. Henry learned about the sub-Saharan gold trade when the Portuguese seized the North African port of Ceuta. He went back to Portugal determined to find a sea route that would bypass the overland caravans through Islamic lands. For more than twenty years, Henry sponsored voyages of discovery along the African coast, searching for gold and for Christian allies against the powerful Islamic states that bordered the Mediterranean. In 1441, his ships returned with tangible rewards in the form of gold dust and African slaves.

The slave trade between Portugal and West Africa grew quickly. After hundreds of years of supplying the Saharan trade caravans, the African slave trade was a well-organized activity when the first Portuguese explorers arrived. Local middlemen brought slaves to the coast, and these middlemen traded with Portuguese merchants for manufactured goods.

At first, the main demand for West African slaves came from newly developed sugar plantations on the Portuguese islands of Madeira and the Azores and from the African states of the Gold Coast. After Christopher Columbus's second voyage across the Atlantic, slave traders found new and bigger markets for slaves in the New World. The slave trade developed into a three-sided Atlantic trade. African slavery was at its heart. Slave ships brought European goods to Africa. Traders used these goods to purchase slaves from Africa. They then carried the slaves across the Atlantic to the Americas. There they were sold to work in gold and silver mines and on plantations. On the third leg of the voyage, ships returned to Europe loaded with precious metals, other raw materials, such as timber and furs, and agricultural products, including sugar, tobacco, and **indigo**.

For more than a hundred years, Portugal had a monopoly on the slave trade. In the sixteenth century, other European powers began to infringe on Portuguese trade routes. For a brief time, the Dutch were the most powerful European power on the West African coast. Yet their dominance was soon challenged by merchants from all over Europe. By the eighteenth century, there was a clear winner in the contest for control of the slave trade: Great Britain.

We end with **abolitionist** efforts to outlaw first the Atlantic slave trade and then slavery itself. The abolition movement began in Britain in the late eighteenth century, inspired by **Enlightenment** ideas about the rights of man and Christian evangelicalism. In spite of its control of the slave trade, Britain was the first country to outlaw the slave trade in 1807. Making the trade illegal did not mean the immediate end of the slave trade or the end of slavery. The profits were too high. It would be 1888 before the last slaves in the Americas were free.

فلا أحسبه سينطبق شزرا ويغلي السعة على فاحلق الحين حلفت ما أغلق

إلا العبد إذا نزرت ثمنه وخفت مؤنته ونزل بمولاه والنحف عليه هواه وأني

ونرجحك هذا الغلام البد بأن أخفف ثمنه عليك من مائتي درهمان شين

شخرى ما جبت فغلته المبلغ في الكأس كما ينفذ في أرخص الغال ولم

Chapter 1

The Advent of the African Slave Trade

An international slave trade existed in Africa long before European explorers and traders arrived on the continent's western coast in the fifteenth century. Arab merchants traded slaves from East Africa across the Indian Ocean to markets on the Red Sea, in the Persian Gulf, and in western India. They sent slaves down the Nile from the eastern Sudan to Egypt. In the west, slaves were forced to walk across the Sahara to the slave markets of North Africa. From there, many slaves were shipped to other parts of the Islamic world.

Scholars estimate ten million Africans traveled across these routes as slaves between 800 and 1900 CE. By comparison, European slavers forced some thirteen million slaves onto the ships that carried them to the Americas.

Opposite: African slaves were sold throughout the Islamic world for centuries before the development of the transatlantic slave trade.

Slavery in the Islamic World

Slavery in the Islamic world was very different from slavery in the Americas and the Caribbean. Race was not an issue. According to Islamic law, it was legal for Muslims to own non-Muslims as slaves, whatever the color of their skin. Slave markets operated throughout the Islamic world, from North Africa and the Middle East to the Ottoman provinces in the Balkans. In these markets, African slaves were sold alongside Turkic slaves from Central Asia, Slavs from Eastern Europe, and Western European slaves. Slaves from Western Europe were taken captive when Barbary pirates seized their ships off the coast of North Africa. Perhaps the most famous example of such a slave is Miguel de Cervantes, the author of *Don Quixote*. He spent five years as a slave in Algiers until he was ransomed.

Unlike most of the slaves in the Americas, few of the Africans who were sold as slaves in the Islamic world worked as field laborers or in mines. Literate slaves, generally from Eastern or Southern Europe, held administrative jobs in government or in wealthy households. Muslim rulers in Egypt, North Africa, and the Middle East used male slaves in their armies or as palace guards. But most slaves were bought to work as servants, entertainers, or harem women in prosperous urban households. This meant Islamic slave markets sold twice as many women as men. The opposite was true in slave markets in the Americas, where most slaves worked in mines or on plantations. Male **eunuchs** were an important exception. They were more expensive than any other type of slave, in part because only one boy in ten survived the brutal operation.

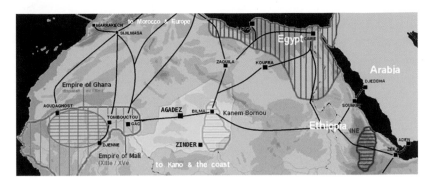

Trade routes across the Sahara desert linked the medieval kingdoms of West Africa with the Mediterranean and the Islamic world.

Under Islamic law, a slave was property. However, every slave was also a person with clearly defined, if limited, rights. A slave owner could sell or give away a slave, but he could not separate slaves from their children. If a slave owner fathered a son with a slave, Islamic law required him to recognize the child as his own and set the boy's mother free. The same law did not apply to daughters. It was not unusual for slave owners to set slaves free in their wills as a religious act of charity.

Muslims did not always follow the laws for the humane treatment of slaves. But the fact that such laws existed meant that, in general, slaves in the Islamic world received better treatment than their counterparts on American plantations. In fact, a few slaves, especially those who worked in the government or the military, rose to positions of great power. Some even owned slaves themselves.

Despite the fact that most Muslim slave owners treated their slaves well by the standards of American plantations, the life of a slave was hard. Most slaves

Trade Routes Across the Sahara

For centuries, the Sahara Desert separated North Africa from sub-Saharan Africa. This region was known at the time as the Sudan, a name that comes from the Arabic for "land of the Blacks." North Africa and sub-Saharan Africa had different economies, social customs, and religions. The first regular trade networks across the desert began after the seventh century, when Arab Muslims brought camels to North Africa. Camels could carry heavier loads than horses or donkeys and travel for long distances without water. They made it possible to cross the great desert that had previously separated the two cultures.

Traveling across the Sahara was a dangerous three-month journey. The trade routes were not roads in any sense of the word, just a string of **oases** separated by long stretches of desert. Oases grew up around sources of water. They were the medieval equivalent of a truck stop. At oases, **caravans** could buy food and supplies and rent fresh camels. At the height of the trade, there were three main routes across the desert. These routes ran from Morocco, Tunis, and Tripoli to the great trading cities on the edge of the Sahara, like Gao, Timbuktu, and Djenne. A fourth route ran from Egypt to the Lake Chad area.

The lure of West African gold led the first Arab traders to travel across the Saharan. North African merchants carried weapons, luxury goods like silk, spices and books from across the Muslim world, horses, and salt purchased from the desert salt mines to sub-Saharan Africa, where they bought gold and slaves. Salt in particular was so valuable that a North African merchant could sell an ounce of salt for an ounce of gold.

Trans-Saharan trade depended on camels, which were brought from the Middle East to North Africa in the seventh century CE.

worked for an average of seven years from the time they were purchased until they died or were set free.

The Saharan Slave Trade

Slavery already existed in sub-Saharan Africa when the Arabs arrived. Some people were enslaved as punishment for a crime or captured during a war with neighboring tribes. Their own families sold some into slavery when food was scarce.

The demand for slaves in Muslim societies changed African slavery into a business. Buying and selling slaves became a regular part of the Saharan trade within a century after the first caravans traveled across the Sahara. By the twelfth century, slave raids were a part of West African life. The medieval kingdom of Kanem, for example, which had nothing else to sell that the traders wanted, regularly raided other tribes to capture slaves. They then traded slaves for the horses and weapons that allowed them to continue their raids. A good horse could cost between ten and thirty slaves, depending on their age, sex, and skills.

Slaves may have been relatively well treated once they reached their final destination in a Muslim household in Tunis or Alexandria, but they suffered as much on the march across the desert as any victim of the transatlantic trade. Caravan leaders took special care of very valuable slaves, such as male eunuchs, beautiful or talented female slaves, or slaves who were sent as a gift from one ruler to another. But most slaves were given less care than the caravan animals. They were chained together and marched long distances through the hot sands. Many carried trade goods on their heads, often more than 30 pounds'

(13.6 kilograms) worth. It took ten slaves to carry the load of one camel. The death rate was high. Slaves who died on the march were left where they fell. Even with the loss of slaves to the hazards of crossing the desert, slave traders earned gross profits as high as 200 percent.

The Saharan slave trade continued with little interruption for well over a thousand years, from the eighth century into the early twentieth century. For much of that time, the Islamic merchants who controlled the trade held a monopoly over both the gold and the slaves of West Africa. That monopoly would be challenged in the fifteenth century when Portuguese explorers landed on the Atlantic coast of Africa in search of gold and Christian allies.

Chapter 2

Exploration, Gold, and African Slaves

European slave traders took their first slaves from the west coast of Africa fifty years before Christopher Columbus sailed across the Atlantic for the first time. Like the North African traders who found their way across the Sahara, the first Europeans to explore the West African coast were looking for gold.

In the late Middle Ages, Europe once again became part of the trading world of the Mediterranean, which was then under Muslim control. Merchants from the Italian city-states of Venice and Genoa opened offices in the main trading cities of Palestine and Egypt. They purchased luxury goods that had traveled a great distance. These goods made their way from China, India, and Indonesia across the silk routes. Traders then shipped them back to Europe.

Opposite: *Tales of Mansa Musa, the fourteenth century ruler of Mali in West Africa, introduced Europeans to sub-Saharan Africa's wealth.*

Europe Becomes Aware of Sub-Saharan Africa

Sub-Saharan gold first came to Europe's attention in 1324 because of Mansa Musa. The ruler of the West African kingdom of Mali, Mansa Musa went on a **pilgrimage** to Mecca. This is known as the **hajj**. The West African king is thought to have traveled with an advance guard of five hundred slaves, many members of his court, and an apparently inexhaustible supply of gold. He carried with him anywhere from one hundred camels to a thousand camels carrying one hundred pounds of gold each. The king built a mosque anywhere he was for Friday prayers. He paid for everything in gold and gave lavish gifts to his hosts. As he passed, beggars lined the streets, hoping they would catch gold nuggets and never have to beg again. Mansa Musa introduced so much gold into local economies that the price of the metal fell in every city he visited. His spending left economic devastation in his wake.

Venetian and Genoese merchants who lived in the Middle East took notice of Mansa Musa's supply of gold. They sent word home about the wealthy king of Mali and his capital, Timbuktu. Trading firms from Venice, Genoa, Granada, and the Flemish markets of the north established new posts in North Africa, in towns such as Marrakech and Fez. There they traded European manufactured goods for the gold dust and bullion that Muslim traders brought across the Sahara.

Setting up trading posts in North Africa brought Europeans merchants closer to the source of sub-Saharan gold. However, it did not eliminate the middleman. European merchants traded with Timbuktu and other West African kingdoms only through North African merchants. They were not allowed to travel into Africa's desert interior—the first European traveler reached Timbuktu in 1828, several centuries after the city's glory days.

Europe's need for gold was growing as its economies rebuilt. By some estimates, two-thirds of that gold came to Europe via camel caravans. If Europeans wanted direct access to West African gold, they needed to find a way to circumvent the Islamic overland trade by sailing around the western coast of Africa. The small state of Portugal led the way. The nation transformed itself in the process from one of the poorest countries in Europe to the owner of a powerful trading empire that stretched from the Iberian Peninsula to western India.

Prince Henry the Navigator and Portuguese Exploration

Prince Henry of Portugal (1394–1460), later known as Prince Henry the Navigator, was the third surviving son of King John of Portugal. He had little hope of inheriting the throne, but was determined to make his mark in the world. In his search for glory and gold, he became the driving force behind the first European attempts to find a sea route around the African coast.

Henry's interest in African trade routes began in 1415. In August of that year, he took part in a Portuguese assault on the Moroccan port of Ceuta. Ceuta was both an important Mediterranean port and the northern end of one of the Saharan caravan routes. The Portuguese took the Muslim stronghold in one day, giving the young prince the moment of glory he sought. It also gave him his first glimpse of African

Prince Henry the Navigator never sailed a ship, but he was responsible for Portugal's development as a maritime power.

riches. When he returned to Ceuta as the Portuguese governor of the city, he learned everything he could about the gold-laden caravans that crossed the Sahara. He went back to Portugal determined to find a sea route that would bypass the overland caravans through Islamic lands: a goal that combined elements of Christian crusades, Portuguese nationalism, economic opportunity, and his desire for personal glory.

Beginning in 1418, Henry sponsored more than fifteen voyages of discovery along the western coast of Africa. Henry's first African expedition was blown out to sea, resulting in the discovery of Madeira, a previously uninhabited island in the Atlantic. For several years, he concentrated his resources on colonizing Madeira and later on conquering and colonizing the Azores islands. At Henry's direction as the absentee governor of the islands, the colonists developed timber, wine, and sugar as export crops. The Portuguese creation of sugar plantations on these Atlantic islands would play an important role in the early growth of the transatlantic slave trade.

Once the colonization of Madeira and the Azores was underway, Henry turned his attention back to the largely unknown coast of Africa. His goal was to find a way around the westernmost point of Africa. This is Cape Bojador, known as the Cape of No Return. Shallow reefs, difficult currents, and changing winds created a popular belief that it was impossible to sail around the cape. And sailors embellished this belief with tales of boiling seas and man-eating monsters.

Henry refused to believe the sailors' tales and continued to send his ships down the West African coast. He required his mariners to keep detailed logbooks and charts. He introduced the use of unfamiliar nautical instruments borrowed from the Islamic world—like the compass, astrolabe, and quadrant. He also encouraged the design of a new, more maneuverable, type of ship, the **caravel**. Taking

Traveling by Caravel Instead of Caravan

The Portuguese developed a new type of ship that transformed European voyages of discovery. The caravel combined features from the Islamic **dhow** and a small, maneuverable vessel used by Portuguese fishermen on the Douro River. The result was a maneuverable ship that was large enough to carry a crew of twenty and their supplies. Instead of using a side-steering oar, the caravel was steered with a rear-mounted rudder. Caravels had between two and four masts. These could be rigged with either square sails or the triangular, slanted **(lateen)** sails of the Arabic dhow, depending on the wind and the currents.

Because the caravel had a **shallow draft**, it was well suited for exploring along unknown coasts and sailing up rivers. Thanks to its lateen sails, it could sail more closely into the wind than earlier square-rigged seagoing ships. This meant the caravel did not have to change direction to cut across the wind as often. As a result, the caravel reduced the time spent at sea. The Portuguese learned they could return to Europe from the equator by sailing westward into the Atlantic for several hundred miles until they reached the point where the prevailing winds would help them instead of sailing north along the coast against the winds.

One of Henry's captains, Venetian mariner Alvise da Cadmosto, described caravels as "The best ships that sailed the seas." Because of its speed and maneuverability, the caravel became the explorer's ship of choice. At least two of Columbus's ships on his first Atlantic voyage were caravels.

Portuguese navigation depended on tools adapted from Muslim innovations, including the caravel, a new style of ship.

the coastal maps used by Mediterranean sailors as a model, scholars hired by Henry made maps of the African coast. Each voyage added to the knowledge gained on the previous expedition.

In 1434, one of Henry's ships, captained by Gil Eames, succeeded in rounding Cape Bojador and returned to Portugal, bringing with him a sprig of rosemary picked on the mainland south of the Cape. Having once passed the Cape of No Return, Henry's expeditions continued south along the Africa coast. In 1441, they reached Cape Blanco, where they raised a tall wooden cross to mark their arrival in the name of Christianity. The next year, they reached Cape Verde. At this point, they had passed the southern boundary of the Sahara and created the possibility of bypassing the Islamic caravan routes. Finally, Henry's expeditions down the coast of Africa began to bring back more tangible rewards than knowledge about ocean currents and Africa's coastal t**opography**.

Portugal Begins the Slave Trade

Portuguese ships brought back small amounts of gold dust and exotic souvenirs, but their most profitable cargo was slaves. In 1441, two of Henry's ships, captained by Antam Gonclaves and Nuño Tristao, landed in a region they named Cape Blanco for its white sands. The area is located on the edge of the desert, in the northern edge of modern Mauritania. At first there seemed to be nothing but sand. However, on the south edge of the cape they found a small market run as a caravan stop by black Africans who had converted to Islam. The Portuguese purchased a small amount of gold dust and some ostrich eggs.

They also seized twelve black Africans to take back to Portugal. They did not capture the Africans to use as slaves. They wanted prove to Prince Henry that they had reached inhabited territory. They also believed the Africans could be a source of knowledge about the geography, politics, and commerce of the African interior. One of the captives was a local chief who spoke some Arabic—the common language of the African trade routes. The chief negotiated for his own freedom and that of a boy from his family, though not for freedom for the other captives. He promised to provide the Portuguese with slaves if they returned him and the boy to their homeland. It was the beginning of the arrangement at the heart of the transatlantic slave trade, in which African leaders provided European traders with slaves.

The following year, Gonclaves returned to Cape Blanco. He brought more gold dust and ten black African slaves back to Portugal. The year after that, a Portuguese expedition returned with some thirty slaves.

The commercial possibilities of the slave trade, even on this small scale, generated new interest in Henry's African expeditions. To this point, he had paid most of the cost of his expeditions himself, with an occasional contribution from the Portuguese royal treasury. Henry had always seen his expeditions in terms of God, gold, and glory. Portuguese businessmen had little interest in investing in dangerous ventures without the chance of profits. When African slaves appeared in the Lisbon markets, they changed their minds. Henry justified the slave trade by claiming that its purpose was to convert the captured pagans to Christianity, thereby saving their souls. The groups of businessmen who put together the money to pay for new slave-trading expeditions were more interested in making money on their investment.

The first organized slave raid occurred in 1444, backed by a group of merchants from Lagos, a port in southern Portugal. An expedition of six Portuguese caravels landed in the islands off the west coast of modern Mauritania with the explicit intention of capturing slaves. The islands were home to poor fishing families who were not equipped to defend themselves against Portuguese sailors armed with guns and swords. The sailors seized 253 Africans—men, women, and children. They killed anyone who resisted. The captives were bound and loaded on the caravels. They remained bound for the six-week-long return voyage under conditions similar to those that the victims of the later Atlantic slave trade would endure.

Their arrival in Lagos was a major public event. Crowds gathered to see the unusual sight of Africans unloaded at the port as if they were cattle. Prince Henry himself arrived to supervise unloading and distributing the human cargo. Forty-six of the best slaves were set aside as Henry's share of the cargo. The rest were divided among the men who invested in the expedition or put up for auction. It was a new experience but one that would be repeated many times. The sugar plantations on Portugal's new Atlantic island possessions needed increasing amounts of labor to meet Europe's growing demand for their products. African slaves provided that labor.

Developing A Slave Trade Network

The Portuguese continued to send slave raids to Africa throughout the mid-1440s. According to court

Portugal built armed trading posts, like the island fortress of Elmina, to defend its trade monopolies in Africa and India.

chronicler Gomes Eanes de Zurara, raiders shipped a total of 927 slaves from West Africa to Portugal between 1445 and 1447.

Raiders moved deeper into the interior beyond the Senegal River. Farther in, they met Africans who were more able to defend themselves than the fishing communities of the western Sahara. Faced with potential slaves who fought back, the Portuguese revised their strategy from raiding to trading. At first, the Portuguese slave trade in Africa did not look much different from the Saharan slave trade. Instead of creating a new trading network, they built on existing African trade networks between interior and coastal communities. Thus, they competed with the Saharan trade caravans for marketable slaves. As was the case in the later transatlantic slave trade, local middlemen brought captives to the coast, where European merchants traded manufactured goods for slaves. They recruited Africans to serve as interpreters and middlemen. In 1456, the king of Portugal sent a representative to negotiate peace treaties with African rulers on the coast. This allowed European traders to build settlements on the coast and travel freely.

The slave trade between Portugal and West Africa grew quickly, soon requiring twenty-five caravels a year. In 1445, Henry built a fort and warehouse on the largest island in Mauritania's Arguin Bay. Arguin Bay served as the most important European gateway into western Africa for more than a hundred years. It was the first of many such overseas trading posts, known as **factories**, to be built along the Portuguese trade routes on the coast of Africa and later in India. These bases served not only as collecting points for trade goods, but as supply stations for Portuguese ships sailing along the coast. Later, they would be defenses against the efforts of other European powers to encroach on their trading monopolies.

Arguin Island was a flourishing trade center, which remained under Portuguese control until 1633 when the Dutch seized it. By 1455, between seven and eight hundred slaves passed through Arguin each year, en route to Portugal or to the Portuguese island colonies of Madeira and the Azores. They also sold slaves to other Africans for gold. Having sailed beyond the control of Muslim middlemen, they became middlemen themselves. Many different kinds of goods traveled up and down their coast in their caravels. Black slaves were an important commodity in the coastal trade, but not the only one.

By the end of the fifteenth century, the African slave trade was a Portuguese institution under royal control. Government administrators oversaw every step of the complicated system that shipped trade goods from across Europe to Africa. Merchants bid for licenses that gave them the right to trade on the African coast. In exchange for licenses, these merchants made payments to the Portuguese crown and made commitments to continue exploration along the unknown African coast. They founded settlements on the mainland with the consent of local rulers. Most notably, they established a massive fortress and warehouse on the Gold Coast, now Ghana. The fortress was named São Jorge da Minta (St. George of the Mine). However, it was commonly known as Elmina, which means "the mine" in Portuguese. It was an appropriate name since in the early sixteenth century, the Gold Coast exported 1,500 pounds (680.3 kg) of gold each year, one-tenth of the world's gold supply.

When caravels returned to Portugal, they delivered their merchandise to the customs house in Lagos. There customs officials inspected the slaves, along with other imported goods, and collected the appropriate import duties before they could be offered for sale.

By the early sixteenth century, almost 200,000 Africa slaves had been transported to Europe and islands in the Atlantic. But slave traders soon found new and bigger market for slaves in the mines and plantations of the New World.

THE GEORGIA NEGRO.
A SOCIAL STUDY
BY
W.E.BURGHARDT DU BOIS.

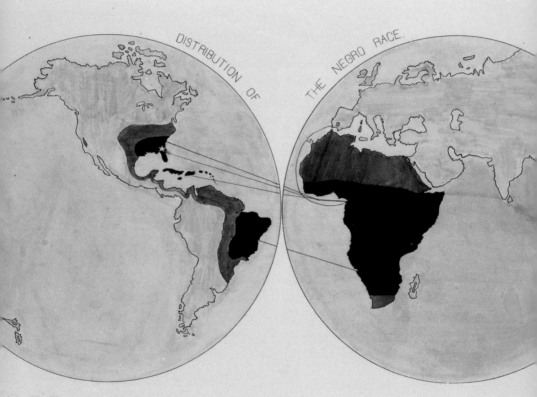

DISTRIBUTION OF THE NEGRO RACE.

≡ ROUTES OF THE AFRICAN SLAVE TRADE.

⊛ THE STATE OF GEORGIA.

THIS CASE IS DEVOTED TO A SERIES OF CHARTS, MAPS AND OT
SIGNED TO ILLUSTRATE THE DEVELOPMENT OF THE AMERICAN NE
TYPICAL STATE OF THE UNITED STATES.

" THE PROBLEM OF THE 20ᵀᴴ CENTURY IS THE PROBLEM OF THE
COLOR—LINE."

Chapter 3

A Triangular Trade

For the first fifty years after Columbus accidentally found his way to the Americas, Portuguese traders who sailed along the coast of West Africa were more interested in gold than slaves. The main demand for slaves from West Africa came from the sugar plantations on the Atlantic islands, owned by Portugal and Spain, and from the African states of the Gold Coast. For much of the sixteenth century, the Gold Coast was a net importer of slaves purchased from Portuguese traders.

The balance between the demand for slaves and gold shifted toward slaves as a result of new slave markets in Latin America. Gold and silver mines were discovered in Hispaniola, Mexico, Brazil, and Peru. These mines produced gold and silver in a quantity and quality the gold fields of Africa could not match and created a perceived need for slave labor. In addition, Europe's growing sweet tooth

Opposite: A small portion of African slaves were sold in the American South. Most landed in Latin America and the Caribbean.

was created by the Atlantic sugar plantations. The desire for more and more sugar led to the creation of sugar plantations in Portuguese Brazil and then in the Caribbean colonies owned by Spain, France, the Netherlands, and Britain. In turn, the spread of sugar plantations fueled an increasingly competitive slave trade. From 1650 to 1850, slaves and human misery were West Africa's primary exports.

The Triangle Trade

The transatlantic slave trade network is often described as the Triangle Trade. In its most basic form, trading ships sailed along three separate legs of a route that began and ended in Europe with stops in West Africa and the New World. European traders brought European trade goods to Africa, which they used to purchase slaves from Arab, Berber, or African traders. They then shipped the slaves across the Atlantic to the mines and plantations of the New World. On the third leg of the trip, ships returned to Europe with agricultural products and raw materials from the Americas, often produced with the labor of slaves sold on previous voyages. On a successful voyage, the ship made a profit at every point of the triangle.

The reality was more complicated. European traders imported goods from India and the Middle East to sell along the coast of West Africa. Some European ships took slaves back to Europe or to the Atlantic islands owned by Portugal and Spain. European traders acted as middlemen between different regions of Africa, carrying both trade goods and slaves from one region to another.

No matter how complex the geographical and commercial relationships became over the course of three hundred years, the Atlantic slave trade was fundamentally a three-sided transaction. Europe, Africa, and the Americas all played a role.

The First Leg of the Triangle: From Europe to Africa

Portugal's trade arrangements with West African merchants established trading patterns that would continue until the slave trade was outlawed in the mid-nineteenth century. European ships arrived with manufactured goods from all across Europe to trade for gold and slaves. Each ship brought an assortment of trade goods that were chosen based on the most recent information regarding the buying habits of African customers at various trading posts. They brought metal goods: knives, hatchets, Spanish swords, iron and copper bars, and large pots made from solid brass that could be melted down and recast by local metal smiths. Brass bracelets from Bavaria were popular. So were glass beads from Venice, mirrors, and conch shells from the Canary Islands. Tobacco and American rum, both products of slave labor on American plantations, arrived in Africa via Europe. These products were traded alongside Dutch gin, French brandy and Portuguese wine. At various times, African markets wanted candles, trumpets, or damask from the workshops of Flanders and France. Guns, which could be used to capture more slaves and expand empires, were a universal favorite.

Cowrie shells from the Indian Ocean, used as currency throughout Africa, were popular trade goods in African slave markets.

In addition to trade goods from Europe, European merchants also imported trade goods for resale from across Asia and other regions of Africa. The Portuguese in particular became skilled at transporting goods from one region of Africa to another. They often replaced Arab traders from North Africa as middlemen. Cowrie shells, which were used as money in West Africa, were imported from as far away as the western coast of India. Printed cotton cloth from northern Nigeria and India was traded along the Slave Coast (western Nigeria, Dahomey and Togo) and the Niger delta. (After the mid-eighteenth century when the Industrial Revolution transformed the British textile industry, cheaper cotton cloth from the factories of Manchester and Birmingham replaced them.) A favorite item in the early days of the slave trade was striped woolen shawls from Tunis.

The European trade goods sold in Africa are sometimes dismissed by historians as cheap trinkets. The implication of this statement is that African consumers were too unsophisticated to judge their worth. But in fact, African merchants established clear rates of exchange for the goods they purchased based on their value in African markets.

The Second Leg of the Triangle: From Africa to the Americas

European merchants purchased luxury items from the forests and plains of Africa: ivory, tropical hardwoods, antelope skins, and ostrich eggs. They bought civet musk, a substance taken from the glands of civet cats that is an ingredient in expensive perfumes. They also bought **gum arabic**, the dried gum of the acacia tress, which was used to make inks, dyes, and medicine. Another popular product was peppery "Guinea grains," which were sold as a substitute for true pepper from the East Indies. But these goods were extras. The trade goods that brought European ships down the African coast were the same as those that drew Arab trade caravans across the Sahara: gold and slaves.

Slaves were chained together into a coffle and marched from the African interior to the shore.

Slaves were typically captured inland by other Africans and marched to the coast. It was a hard trip over rough terrain that lasted days, and sometimes weeks. The captives were burdened by the weight of the iron chains used to link them together. As many as half of them died from exhaustion and starvation along the way.

Once at the coast, slaves were sold to European buyers. In the early days of the slave trade, the buyers were agents of European trading companies, who worked at the company's permanent trading posts on the African coast. These agents held the slaves at the trading post until the next slave ship arrived, often for long periods of time under horrible conditions. Each slave ship, which belonged to the same company as the trading post, delivered a cargo of trade goods and picked up a cargo of slaves. The agent at the trading

The Columbian Exchange

The Atlantic trade brought about unexpected changes in the way people lived. One of the most important of these was the transformation of diets in Europe, Asia, and Africa. This shift was a result of new foods from the Americas, first described by historian Alfred Crosby in his groundbreaking book, *The Columbian Exchange* (1972). The most important of these new foods was the potato. Potatoes could be planted in fallow fields, produced more food per acre than existing grain crops, and could be stored in the ground. For much of Europe, the introduction of the potato meant a better diet for the poor and a reduced chance of famine.

The potato was not the only New World food to change Old World diets. Tomatoes, chilies, sweet peppers, beans, and squash made themselves at home in the kitchens of Europe and Asia. So did both vanilla and chocolate. Peanuts and maize, known in the United States as corn, became major crops in Africa.

The introduction of new foods did not flow in one direction. Slave ships also carried African foods to the new world. By the early 1700s, slave traders had learned their captives were more likely to survive the voyage across the Atlantic if they were fed familiar foods. Slave ships began to stock plantains, rice, limes, sorghum, mille, cassava, and, most importantly, yams as provisions for slaves. The rule of thumb for provisioning slave ships for the trip across the Atlantic was two hundred yams per slave.

post then used the new trade goods to purchase more slaves.

By the late seventeenth century, individual slave ships financed by groups of businessmen replaced the large trading companies. The captain of a slave ship would trade directly with African slave traders, often buying small groups of slaves from several different markets along the coast.

From the Americas Back to Europe

When a slave ship arrived in the Americas, after up to two months at sea, ship captains brought their slaves to market as quickly as possible. If the ship's owners had an agent in the colonies, the slaves would be delivered to him. If not, the captain would usually sell his human cargo as a group to a local slave dealer. In some cases, a colonial merchant or group of merchants would contract with slave traders in Lisbon, Amsterdam, or London to buy slaves at a set price and would take delivery on arrival. A few captains sold slaves directly to plantation and mine owners.

Once they disposed of their slaves, ship captains loaded their ships for the return voyage to Europe with agricultural products and raw materials. Gold, silver, and sugar were always the most important products shipped from the Americas to Europe. Between the years 1500 and 1800, Latin American mines produced as much as 220 million pounds (99.8 million kg) of silver and 5.5 million pounds (2.5 million kg) of gold. Annual exports of sugar from the Americas to Europe rose from about 66 million pounds (29.9 million kg) in the mid-seventeenth century to almost 2 billion pounds (900 million kg) two hundred years later.

Sugar was not the only slave-produced export from the Americas. Plantations in Brazil and the West Indies exported cotton, cocoa, and coffee. Tobacco became a staple export crop for Virginia and Maryland. The Carolinas produced rice and indigo. Farther north, colonies shipped fish, furs, and forest products. Rhode Island transformed sugar from the Caribbean into molasses and rum.

The Atlantic slave trade stood at the center of a complex international economy that linked Europe, Africa, and the Americas. At first, Portugal stood unchallenged at the center of the Atlantic trade network. But by the end of the fifteenth century, another European power threatened Portugal's monopoly.

Chapter 4

Slave Traders, Slave Owners, and Slaves

The major players in most trade routes can be broken down into three groups: the people who supplied goods at one end of the route, the people who transported goods along the route, and the people who bought goods at the other end of the route. In the case of the transatlantic slave networks, a fourth group must be considered: the slaves themselves.

African Suppliers

After hundreds of years of the Saharan trade caravans, the African slave trade was a well-organized activity when the first Portuguese explorers arrived. The Portuguese quickly learned it was more profitable to buy slaves than to capture

Opposite: Many of the slaves sold in the New World worked in the gold and silver mines in Hispaniola, Mexico, and Brazil.

The coast of West Africa, based on the work of fifteenth century cartographer Martin Behaim

them. After the mid-fifteenth century, European slave traders seldom captured Africans as slaves. Most Africans sold in the Atlantic slave trade were purchased from other Africans.

When the Portuguese first arrived, most political entities on the West African coast were small: only 1,000–2,000 square miles (2,590–5,180 sq. km) in size. Many were centered on a single city or large village, similar to the city-states of ancient Mesopotamia or classical Greece.

The interior of Africa was a different matter. The Songhai Empire ruled over most of the western Sudan. It was the largest and last of the great pre-colonial empires of West Africa. Like the Mali and Ghanaian empires that preceded it, the Songhai controlled the trade between West and North Africa, including the supply of slaves to the Saharan slave trade. The Songhai capital city was Gao: a vast unwalled city with a population of 100,000 people—the same size as Lisbon at the time. It was home to rich markets where merchants sold salt from the Sahara, European horses, cloth from Venice, spices from Indonesia, swords, spurs, and bridles. Slaves were sold in a separate market. The Songhai boasted that a raid to the south could bring back a thousand slaves in a single day.

Over the course of the Atlantic slave trade, kingdoms and tribes rose and fell, expanded and consolidated. Scholars have identified at least 173 different political groups in West Africa at the time the Portuguese arrived, including 68 organized nations and 45 distinct ethnic groups, each with their own history, government, customs and languages. One thing they had in common was their involvement in the slave trade.

Some people were condemned to slavery as punishment for crimes, but most slaves sold to European traders were captured in a war or a slave raid. The line between the two was thin. Wars often began when members of one group raided neighboring nations or villages in order to obtain captives who could be sold as slaves. Such raids could turn into a war of retaliation, leading to more slaves for both sides. As the market for slaves grew, so did the number of wars between African groups. Like the North African merchants before them, European traders made these wars easier by selling guns and gunpowder to African leaders.

In regions where there was no strong state, African merchants acquired slaves through kidnapping rather than warfare. Anyone found alone in an isolated place was easy prey for slave takers. Even in states where kidnapping was illegal, kidnapping victims were easy to sell. Most slave traders were willing to buy anyone, whether or not that person was a legal slave by African standards.

Slave Traders

Portugal enjoyed a monopoly on exporting slaves from Africa from 1440 to the 1590s. The Portuguese used armed force to protect the trade routes down the African coast to Elmina. The Portuguese similarly protected the even more profitable sea routes that continued past Elmina and around the southern tip of Africa to the Spice Islands of Indonesia. Portuguese sailors who gave information about the trade routes to foreigners were severely punished. The powerful Portuguese navy seized foreign ships caught sailing toward the Indies and their crews were sentenced to a lifetime in the galleys. This punishment equated to slavery of a different kind.

Armed factories—part trading post and part fortress—were critical to fending off rival European merchants. They also helped ensure the Portuguese government received the taxes owed on every trading ship that went in and out of Africa. By the end of the fifteenth century, a chain of armed posts stretched from the first post at Arguin Island to the South China Sea.

Portugal's monopoly of the slave and spice trades was challenged at the end of the sixteenth century when a new player entered the field. The small Protestant states of the Netherlands were determined to challenge Portugal's monopoly for religious and business reasons.

The Rapid Rise and Fall of the Dutch West Indies Company

Dutch ships first appeared on the West African coast in the 1590s. The Netherlands had been at war with Spain since 1568, when the Protestant states rebelled against Catholic rule. When Phillip II of Spain conquered Portugal in 1580, the Portuguese overseas empire became a tempting target for the Dutch.

The first Dutch trading companies were organized to trade in the Pacific and Indian Oceans. However, they recognized the potential gains that could be earned in the West African trade. By 1608, the United Dutch East Indian Company (VOC) claimed to have twenty ships operating along the West African coast. But between the 1590s and the 1620s, Dutch activity in Africa—including the slave trade—was sporadic. Africa remained secondary to the VOC's main interest, which was the Asian trade.

In 1621, the Dutch government chartered a new **joint-stock company**: the Dutch West Indies Company. The **charter** gave the new company a monopoly in the West African and American trade, putting it in direct competition with the Portuguese. At first, the company's ships raided Portuguese slave ships and then smuggled the pirated slaves into Latin America's slave markets. The Dutch slave trade continued on a small scale until the 1630s, when they seized northern Brazil from the Portuguese. They now owned a plantation colony, which meant they needed African slaves to work their own sugarcane fields. In order to ensure their supply, they built their own armed factories on the West African coast. They also seized Portuguese strongholds, beginning with Elmina in 1637. Over the course of five years, they drove the Portuguese from their factories at Luanda, São Tome, Annabon, São Paula, and Beneguela. When they seized Axim in 1642, the Dutch became the dominant European power on the West African coast.

While the Dutch successfully displaced the Portuguese in the West African trade, they did not succeed in replicating Portugal's monopoly over that trade. Merchants from all over Europe shouldered their way into the slave trade, first as **privateer**s and later as the representatives of chartered trading companies.

The British Take Over the Atlantic Slave Trade

The British slave trade began in 1562 with an act of piracy. Captain John Hawkins sailed from London with three ships and the intention of breaking into the Atlantic slave trade. He stopped at the Canary Islands.

British privateer Sir John Hawkins (1532–1595) seized slaves from Portuguese ships and smuggled them into Spanish American colonies.

There he hired a pilot to help him navigate the waters of the African coast. When he reached the Guinea Coast, he captured some three hundred Africans—most seized from Portuguese slave boats. He then sailed across the Atlantic to Hispaniola (now the Dominican Republic and Haiti). Spain maintained tight control over who could sell slaves in the American colonies and at what price. Hawkins got around the law by pretending he needed to make repairs to his ship. He claimed he needed to sell slaves on the black market in order to pay for the necessary materials and services. (This ruse would become a standard ploy for traders who wanted to smuggle slaves into Spanish America.)

Hawkins's expedition set the pattern for the British slave trade for the next hundred years. The British government licensed privateers to attack Portuguese and Spanish ships as part of the ongoing war between Spain and the Protestant states of Britain and the Netherlands. Privateers seized Portuguese slave ships, smuggled slaves into the Spanish colonies, and captured Portuguese and Spanish ships returning from Brazil and the Caribbean with sugar and precious metals.

British involvement in the slave trade changed in the seventeenth century with the establishment of British colonies in the Caribbean. At first, plantation owners bought slaves from Dutch traders. In 1660, King Charles II granted a charter to The Company of Royal Adventurers into Africa, a joint-stock company intended to rival the Dutch West Indies Company. The company was headed by the king's younger brother, the Duke of York (later King James II). Its charter gave the company a monopoly on British trade to West Africa and the slave trade to Britain's American colonies for a thousand years. The company was reorganized with a new charter as the Royal African Company in 1672. Between 1660 and 1689, the

British company exported ninety thousand slaves to the Americas, at least half of whom went to Barbados and Jamaica.

The Royal African Company lost its royal patronage and its monopoly in 1688 after the Glorious Revolution ended the Stuart monarchy. With trade now open, individual slave ships entered the trade, financed by small groups of merchants in London, Bristol, and Liverpool. The number of slaves transported on British ships increased to more than twenty thousand a year. By the early eighteenth century, Britain was the largest slave trading country in the world.

Slave Traders from North America

The biggest customers for slaves in Britain's American colonies were in the Caribbean or the American South. However, most of the merchants who shipped slaves from Africa were located in the North.

Newport, Rhode Island, was the first and most important North American port to figure in the Atlantic slave trade. Newport had strong ties to the sugar and molasses producers of Barbados. The port also boasted a thriving shipbuilding industry and rum distilleries. Beginning in 1723, the city's merchants shipped rum directly to Africa. They therefore bypassed British middlemen to create their own version of the triangular trade with Africa and the Caribbean. Other American ports participated in the trade, including Providence, Boston, New York, Philadelphia, and Baltimore.

Congress made it illegal to import slaves in 1807. Yet New York remained a major hub for illegal slave shipping. The last slave-ship captain was arrested months before the beginning of the American Civil War in 1861.

Slave Markets

In the United States, we tend to think of the slave trade in terms of the American South. In fact, North America was a small player in the trade. Fewer than half a million slaves were sent to North America between 1619 and 1863, when President Abraham Lincoln signed the Emancipation Proclamations. The majority of the estimated thirteen million slaves taken across the Atlantic from Africa went to Latin America and the Caribbean.

Portuguese and Spanish Colonies

On January 22, 1510, King Ferdinand of Spain approved sending fifty slaves to work in the Hispaniola gold mines: "the best and strongest available." Three weeks later, he ordered another two hundred slaves sent to Santo Domingo for sale as soon as possible. It was the beginning of the slave trade to the Americas.

By the mid-sixteenth century, the Spanish empire in the New World depended on slavery. The same was true of Portuguese Brazil. Both mines and plantations needed large work forces able to do backbreaking manual labor. At first the colonists tried to use Native Americans as forced labor, but many died and those who survived often fled into the countryside. Colonists solved their labor shortage by importing slaves from Africa, who found it difficult to disappear into the local population. By 1619, European ships had carried a million African slaves to the New World.

Spanish merchants were not directly involved in the slave trade. Instead the Spanish government sold monopoly contracts, called ***asientos***, which gave purchasers the right to import a specific number of slaves at a specific price to the Spanish colonies. At first, the Portuguese had a monopoly on transporting slaves to Latin America. But as other European countries entered the slave trade, the *asiento* was sold to the highest bidder. With the exception of the slave trade, the Spanish government did not allow direct trade between its colonies and foreign merchants. Slave traders were willing to pay a high price for the *asiento* because it gave them the possibility of smuggling other goods into Latin America's lucrative colonial markets. In fact, the *asiento* was so valuable that in 1713, it was assigned as part of a peace treaty between Spain and Britain.

British Colonies Enter the Triangle Trade

The first African slaves arrived in North America in Jamestown, Virginia, in 1619—a year before the Puritans landed in Massachusetts—carried by a Dutch privateer. The crew had previously seized the cargo of a Spanish vessel, including twenty-some African slaves. The ship needed supplies, so the Dutch traded the Africans for food.

These first slaves seem to have been treated as if they were **indentured servants**, which was the primary labor model in Britain's North American colonies for the first half of the seventeenth century. Slaves were expensive and ongoing hostilities between Britain and Spain limited the British colonies' access to slaves. At the same time, Britain experienced a population explosion between 1500 and the mid-1600s that left thousands unemployed and homeless. Many colonists arrived as indentured servants, who paid for their passage to the New World by working without pay for four to seven years. By 1625, between 35

The Interesting Narrative of Olaudah Equiano

Most accounts of the slave trade were written by traders or by people dedicated to abolishing the slave trade. Though the slaves themselves wrote few accounts, one important exception is *The Interesting Narrative of Olaudah Equiano*, published in 1789.

Olaudah Equiano was born in 1745 in what is now Nigeria. When he was ten or eleven, he was kidnapped and sold as a slave in Barbados, but he did not remain in Barbados long. He was sold first to a planter in Virginia and three months later to a British naval officer. He spent most of his time as a slave working on British slave ships and naval vessels. One of his owners, Henry Pascal, the captain of a British trading ship, gave Equiano the name Gustavas Vassa, which he used for most of his life.

In 1762, Equiano was sold to Robert King, a Quaker merchant from Philadelphia. King allowed Equiano to trade small amounts of merchandise on his own behalf. He earned enough money to buy his freedom in 1766.

Once free, Equiano settled in England, where he worked as a merchant and became active in the abolition movement there. At the urging of his abolitionist friends, he wrote a memoir describing his capture and his experiences as a slave. *The Interesting Narrative of Olaudah Equiano, or Gustavus Vassa the African, Written by Himself* became a best seller in England.

Olaudah Equiano (1745–1797) purchased his freedom. His memoir of his life as a slave became an eighteenth-century bestseller.

and 40 percent of the colonial population were indentured servants.

Over time, the supply of new indentured servants was not large enough to meet the labor demand. Planters looked for other sources of plantation labor. Like the Spanish, they tried without success to press Native Americans into service. As a result, race-based slavery was introduced into the North American colonies over the course of the seventeenth century. In 1641, Massachusetts became the first of Britain's North American colonies to recognize slavery as a legal institution. Georgia was the last to legalize slavery in 1760.

At first, the number of slaves in North America was relatively small. Together, Virginia, Maryland, and the Carolinas imported roughly ten thousand slaves between 1670 and 1700. But the plantation economies grew. In addition to tobacco, colonists began to grow sugar, rice, and cotton. The labor demand increased throughout the eighteenth century. Between 1787 and 1808, ninety thousand slaves were shipped into South Carolina alone.

The Slaves Themselves

The slaves who were sold across the Atlantic trade routes were unwilling and virtually silent participants in the transatlantic slave trade. Roughly 80 percent of the people who arrived in the Americas between 1500 and 1820 were African slaves.

Their experiences were horrific. Taken from their homes, often by violence, they trekked across rough terrain from the interior to the coast, chained together by the neck into a line, known as a **coffle**. Once at the coast, they were stripped, shaved, and branded. Some were loaded onto a waiting ship. Others were imprisoned in a company factory until the next slave-ship arrived. Most had never seen the sea, a ship, or a white man before. Rumors spread that their captors were monsters or cannibals. Thrown together with people from different parts of Africa, many did not have even the comfort of a shared language with their fellow prisoners.

Once a ship was fully loaded, it began the long voyage across the Atlantic, known as the **Middle Passage**. The voyage took two to three months; bad weather could make the trip longer. During the trip across the Atlantic, slaves were packed in the hold, except for brief periods of exercise in good weather. Male slaves were chained together, sometimes so closely they could not move. Women and children were considered less of a threat so were left unfettered.

It was in the ship captain's interest to deliver as many slaves as possible at the journey's end, but enough slaves died on each voyage that slave-ships were sometimes described as coffins. When a ship was becalmed and food ran short, or if disease broke out among the captives, the death rates skyrocketed for crew and slaves alike.

After they arrived at a port in New World, slaves endured one last journey. Sold at auction or delivered to a prearranged buyer, parted from their families and their shipmates, many traveled by foot to the plantations or mines where they would be put to work. Most would survive for seven to ten years, enduring a life of hard labor before dying far from home.

EUROPEAN
HALL
OF
DELIBERATION

CONGO
ATROCITIE
DEBATE
PROCEEDING
TILL FURTHER
NOTICE

THE GUILT OF DELAY.

Congo Slave-Driver. "I'M ALL RIGHT. THEY'RE STILL TALKING."

Chapter 5

The Effects of the Transatlantic Slave Trade

Transatlantic trade linked together regions that had previously been separate, creating a truly global economy for the first time. The slave trade provided the labor and produced the investment capital that made the larger Atlantic trade possible. In the process, it transformed both African and European economies, disrupted African societies, and shaped the composition and culture of the colonial North and South Americas. The cost in terms of human suffering was horrific.

The Slave Trade's Effect on African Economies and Societies

It is impossible to talk about the slave trade's effect on Africa in monolithic terms. Pre-colonial Africa was a more complicated place than early modern

Opposite: Treatment of Africans in colonies like the Belgian Congo was often as brutal as that suffered by African slaves.

Europe. It was not only vast in size, but it included a wide range of ecological zones and a large and changing number of political entities. There was not one "Africa" any more than there was one "Europe." Different groups had different social structures, cultural traditions, languages, and religions.

Not all Africans suffered personally from the slave trade. The trade gave rise to new classes of wealthy merchants and warlords. Many of the warlords owed their power to exporting slaves and accumulating luxury goods, which they could use to reward their followers and increase their political influence. Coastal traders profited from the sale of European trade goods to the interior. Rulers at every stage of the supply chain imposed taxes on the trade. European traders introduced Africans to new commercial goods from Europe and Asia and new food crops from across the Mediterranean and Asia as well as the Americas. The cash economy expanded. The only thing that didn't change over the course of three hundred years was the trail of human misery.

Population Loss

Today most scholars agree some thirteen million Africans were forced into slavery in the Americas over three centuries. If you take into account those who died on the trek to the coast or during the Middle Passage across the Atlantic, the number of Africans lost to the slave trade may have been closer to thirty million.

This direct population loss is not the full story. The loss of millions of Africans slowed population growth. Slave traders purchased only those who were young, strong, and healthy. Their loss indirectly affected birth rates. In addition, since most of the captives sent across the Atlantic were male, some areas of West Africa were left with a shortage of men. At least one scholar, African historian Boubacar Barry, argues those who were left behind were more vulnerable to famine and less able to defend themselves against violence. Scholar Patrick Manning calculates that if slaves had not been forced to emigrate, the population of Africa as a whole would have totaled 100 million in 1850 instead of 50 million. The effect of this loss of productive labor on Africa's economic development is impossible to calculate. Some argue the continent still hasn't recovered.

The Rise and Fall of African States

Involvement in the Atlantic slave trade created new kingdoms and destroyed old ones. The slave trade encouraged African states to go to war more frequently, which in turn increased the number of captives taken who could be sold as slaves. Some large states and political confederations such as the kingdoms of Jolof or Kongo, broke apart into new, smaller states. This was a direct result of increased wars between kingdoms and the disruption caused by civil wars. One of these new states was the Portuguese colony of Angola, which was founded in the sixteenth century in Kongo territory in exchange for helping the ruler of Kongo defend his country against invasion by another African ruler. Angola was one of the last European colonies to win its independence. It became the independent Republic of Angola in 1975.

Riches obtained from the sale of slaves gave some kingdoms, especially those on the coast, the resources

A seventeenth-century map of Africa, attributed to Dutch cartographer Joducus Hondius (1563–1612)

to expand their territory. In the seventeenth century, two large powerful states rose as a result of large-scale slave trading: Dahomey in the Bight of Benin and Asante on the Gold Coast. The slave trade was so central to Dahomey's economy that its rulers remained involved in the trade throughout the nineteenth century in spite of British pressure to abolish it. At least one ruler of Dahomey argued the British should not expect them to abandon the trade without offering an equally lucrative source of revenue to replace it. Taken together, the compensation offered by the British and the development of palm oil production did not come close to replacing Dahomey's slave trade profits.

Slavery Within Africa

One of the most important and long-lasting consequences of the Atlantic slave trade was the expansion of slavery within Africa. Slavery existed in various forms before the Portuguese arrived. However, the number of slaves was relatively small and slavery was primarily domestic in nature. Ironically, slavery in Africa increased after Britain and the United States outlawed the transatlantic slave trade. Slaves went from being a trade good to being a vital element in African production. By the end of the nineteenth century, there were five to six million slaves in Africa. Like their counterparts in the American plantations, they produced agricultural commodities for international markets. These included grain, indigo, cloves, peanuts, and palm oil.

Africa's internal slave trade stopped with the "scramble for Africa," when European imperial powers seized control of large portions of the African continent. European colonial governments stopped Africans from raiding for slaves and selling them in open markets. However, they did nothing to free those already enslaved. As late as the 1920s, millions of people in Africa were still slaves.

The Slave Trade's Role in the Industrial Revolution

At its height, the slave trade was a critical element in a global trading system that linked Africa, America, Asia, and Europe together, with Europe as the economic center. On the eve of the American Revolution, commodities produced by African slaves made up one-third of the value of European commerce.

measured precisely. That said, we know that there were direct links. British manufacturers produced inexpensive copper goods, glassware, and cotton textiles designed especially for the African market. Trading networks on the African coasts and in the Caribbean purchased British goods in enormous amounts. By the last quarter of the eighteenth century, the Africa trade accounted for one-third of Manchester's textile production. Slaves purchased with Manchester fabrics were shipped to the Caribbean and the American South. There they were often clothed in fabric made in Britain. Slave-produced cotton was shipped back to Britain. As a result, British textile factories produced cotton goods more cheaply than their competitors in India, where the finest hand-woven cotton of the time was made. Textiles were not the only British industry to profit from the slave trade. Sugar refineries in London, Bristol, and Liverpool and tobacco-related industries in Glasgow also depended on the slave trade triangle.

Historians debate how profitable the slave trade was for Britain as a whole—just as they debate whether imperialism was profitable. But there is no doubt that many Britons made a living from the trade. Merchant families made—and lost—fortunes investing in slave trade voyages. (Profits varied from voyage to voyage, but returns on investment averaged between 8 and 10 percent in the second half of the eighteenth century.) The slave trade was a key part of Britain's extensive maritime trade industry in the eighteenth century: one-third to one-half of the ships that sailed out of Liverpool were related to the slave trade in one form or another. It provided work for ship owners and builders, sail and rope makers, customs

J. M. W. Turner's painting The Slave Ship *(1840) was originally titled* Slavers Throwing Overboard the Dead and Dying *— a common practice.*

officials, dock laborers and seaman, **chandlers**, and nautical-instrument makers. The shipping trade also contributed to the growth of new business institutions, including banks and marine and fire insurance. Maritime policies covered the loss of slaves and other cargo due to perils of the sea. But by 1748, most standard marine policies excluded coverage for slaves who died of natural causes while in transit or for damage caused to the ship or cargo as a result of a slave insurrection.

The growth of shipping and the slave trade contributed to Britain's overall prosperity. Many businessmen reinvested profits from the slave trade and other imperial ventures. They invested not only in more slave voyages but in agricultural improvements, canals, textile factories, and other forms of manufacturing. The slave trade reached beyond British ports. In the rural areas surrounding each slave port, manufacturers, merchants, and farmers benefited by providing trade goods and supplies for outgoing slave ships. So many people profited from the slave trade—directly and indirectly—that people from all levels of society were ready to lobby in defense of the slave trade when abolitionists began the fight to end the trade in the 1780s.

The abolition of the slave trade in 1808 did not end Britain's participation. British ships could no longer carry slaves, but British merchants and manufacturers provided their goods to slave traders of other nationalities well into the nineteenth century.

Changing Europe from the Inside Out

African slaves in the Americas produced commodities that changed how Europeans lived. Tobacco, coffee, cotton, sugar, and, to a lesser extent, chocolate became everyday staples. Sugar was the most important of these and the one most closely linked to the transatlantic slave trade.

Sugarcane first reached Europe with returning crusaders in the twelfth century. It was classified as a spice. And like other spices from Asia, it was a luxury enjoyed primarily by the wealthy.

The Portuguese were the first to use slave labor to man sugar plantations. When Prince Henry sent colonists to Madeira in 1425, they carried sugarcane with them. By the 1490s, Madeira was one of the leading producers of sugar in Europe, with two hundred plantations, eighty sugar mills, and two thousand African slaves working in the cane fields. But sugar remained a luxury.

Sugar's status as a luxury item changed after sugar production became an important part of colonial economies. Sugarcane plants crossed the Atlantic with Columbus in 1493. The first shipment of American sugar arrived in Spain in 1517—produced by some of the first slaves shipped to the Americas. In total, roughly 70 percent of the slaves who landed in the Americas worked on sugar plantations. First planted by the Spanish in Santo Domingo, sugar became the primary cash crop for Spanish, Dutch, and British colonies throughout the Caribbean and in Portuguese Brazil. As more sugar was planted, processed, and shipped back to Europe, the price fell. What had once been available only to the wealthy became affordable to virtually everyone.

By the mid-seventeenth century, sugar had made the leap from luxury to necessity, particularly in Britain. In 1700, the average Englishman ate 4 pounds (1.8 kg) of American-grown sugar a year. By 1900, that amount had increased to 100 pounds (45.3 kg). The slave trade had transformed Britain's eating habits—and ruined many citizens' teeth.

Building the Americas

Between 1492 and 1820, 80 percent of the people who embarked for the Americas were African slaves. Most of them were taken to Latin America and the Caribbean. Brazil was the destination for more than one-third. From different nationalities themselves, they were sold to owners in colonies owned by Britain, France, the Netherlands, Portugal, and Spain. The experiences of a slave in the seventeenth century French colony of St. Domingue differed from those of a slave in eighteenth-century Virginia or nineteenth-century Brazil—at least in the details. Despite these differences, when we look for the African roots of American cultures we find common experiences.

The exploitation of African labor fueled the growth of the Americas. Most of the large-scale economic enterprises in the American colonies depended on the labor of African slaves. They mined gold in Brazil and silver in Mexico. They worked in the sugarcane fields in Brazil and the Caribbean. They raised cattle and cocoa in the area that is now Venezuela, and indigo in the Caribbean, Louisiana, and South Carolina. They grew rice in South Carolina and Virginia and, by the eighteenth century, raised cotton throughout the American South. The silver mines at Potosí, in what is now Bolivia, were the only important exception. They relied on forced labor from the local population.

African slaves and the slave trade made significant contributions to the economies of all the American colonies, on plantations and off. The demands of the triangle trade encouraged the production of molasses in the Caribbean and rum in Rhode Island. Slaves worked as domestic servants and skilled tradesmen from New England to Chile. They built ships in Havana and worked on the docks in New York City.

Beyond their forced economic contribution, the massive presence of African slaves and their descendants was central to the creation of American cultures. Torn from their homes, they were often separated from each other by different ethnic backgrounds, religions, and languages. In fact, some scholars suggest that they did not think of themselves as *African* at all until they were thrown together in the New World. Thrust into an alien and hostile environment, people from different parts of Africa created new and diverse cultures from a combination of African, European, and American elements. In Latin American countries, African slaves and their descendants were an exploited majority, divided by a complex hierarchy of race-based gradations. In North America, African slaves and their descendants were a visible minority. Whether the majority or minority, African slaves wove their languages, religions and traditions into the New World's evolving culture.

The question of who benefited from the slave trade is a complicated one. Historians continue to argue whether the slave trade was profitable to the European countries that controlled it and whether the slave trade was responsible for the current condition of Africa. They attempt to dissect the relationship between the slave trade and industrial revolution, to understand the cultural differences between Spain and Britain's economic response to colonial wealth, to uncover the often-forgotten involvement of Massachusetts, New York, Pennsylvania, and Rhode Island in the triangle trade and to consider differences between the slave-trading kingdoms of Africa.

No one argues over who the biggest losers were. The most obvious effect of the Atlantic slave trade was human suffering and degradation on a massive scale. Conditions for the enslaved were horrendous at every step of the trade—from the march to the coast to the American mines and plantations. Even after slavery was abolished, it left behind an underclass of people of African descent throughout the Americas and a heritage of racism.

Chapter 6

The End of the Transatlantic Slave Trade

The transatlantic slave trade was not abolished with a single historical act. Instead, the trade ended one country at a time in a series of individual acts of abolition and rebellion across the Atlantic trading network. These began with the Haitian Revolution in 1791 and ended with Brazil's abolition of slavery in 1888.

In the eighteenth century, when the slave trade was at its height, the philosophical and scientific movement known as the Enlightenment challenged traditional assumptions about social institutions. In the writings of thinkers such as John Locke, Voltaire, Rousseau, and Diderot, slavery became the metaphor for everything that was wrong with power relations in eighteenth-century society. Freedom appeared as the highest political value. But though

Opposite: Jean-Jacques Dessalines participated in the Haitian slave rebellion in 1791 and later became the emperor of Haiti. Following the end of the revolution in 1804, he called for the massacre of French residents.

Enlightenment thinkers spoke out in favor of the rights of man, they did not necessarily apply the concept of freedom to African slaves. In fact, Locke, whose ideas on law and natural rights would inspire the founders of the American Revolution, invested £600 in the Royal African Company. In 1787, when the question of slavery came up in debates surrounding the creation of the United States' Constitution, political consensus won out over principle. In the end, the impulse to abolish slavery and the slave trade would come from two very different sources: the slaves themselves and members of Britain's radical religious groups.

Slave Resistance

African slave resistance movements began almost as soon as slaves arrived in the Americas. The first slave rebellion occurred on Hispaniola in 1522, twelve years after the delivery of the first slaves to the Spanish colony. The bloody uprising was followed by many others over the centuries.

Other slaves chose flight rather than fight. Runaway slaves, called **"maroons"** from the Spanish *cimarrón*, meaning savage, formed their own communities in uninhabited wilderness areas. There they could not easily be attacked by soldiers or slave hunters. Most maroons concentrated on survival. Alternatively, some engaged in guerrilla warfare against neighboring plantations and helped other slaves escape. The most successful maroon communities negotiated treaties with nearby colonial settlements.

In the eighteenth century, fueled in part by the example of the American and French revolutions, slave resistance escalated. The largest, bloodiest, and most

Dominique-François Toussaint Louverture (1743–1803) turned rebellious slaves into a formidable military force.

important of these slave uprisings began in 1791. It took place in the French colony of St. Domingue, located on the western half of the island of Hispaniola. The European powers considered the island the jewel of the Caribbean. It produced 30 percent of the world's sugar and more than half of its coffee, accounting for more than one-third of France's foreign trade. The colony was the largest single market for the Atlantic slave trade. With a population of roughly half a million slaves, it had the largest slave population in the Caribbean.

There had been hints of slave unrest for a long time. Maroon communities raided plantations throughout the 1780s, and there were several small revolts prior to 1791. In August 1791, slaves from many plantations joined forces in an uprising that swept across the island. As the revolt continued, it acquired a talented leader, François Dominique Toussaint (1742–1803) a **freedman** of African descent who was himself a slave owner. Many slaves were inspired by the American and French revolutions, which were in turn inspired by Enlightenment political theories. These men and women fought not only for their personal freedom, but for their country's independence from France. Toussaint, who soon took the surname Louverture ("the opening"), turned rebel slaves into a formidable military force that repeatedly defeated both French and British forces. Europeans were stunned by the skill and determination with which they fought. Modern historian John Thornton suggests they had fought before. Most of Toussaint's troops were African-born and seasoned veterans who were captured as slaves while fighting in wars on the Angola-Congo coast.

In 1804, St. Dominigue became the independent nation of Haiti, with a government run by former slaves.

Britain Abolishes the Slave Trade

The first popular movement for the abolition of the slave trade began in England in the late eighteenth century. The Society of Friends, also known as the Quakers, were the first group to take a public stand against slavery and the slave trade. Surprisingly, Quakers had been prominent slave traders in the seventeenth century and American Quakers had owned slaves since the founding of Pennsylvania in 1681. By the 1770s, the Quaker church took the position that all slaves should be freed. In fact, some congregations excommunicated Quakers who continued to own slaves.

The Quakers found natural allies for their campaign to abolish slavery in a group of wealthy businessmen. This group was mockingly known by their contemporaries as the Saints, and later called the Clapham Sect. The members of the Clapham Sect were **evangelical** Christians whose beliefs emphasized personal salvation and a commitment to principles of individual and social responsibility. They called their beliefs "practical humanity."

Both groups focused on what today we call **grassroots organizing**. They collected and published information condemning the slave trade, including *The Interesting Narrative of Olaudah Equiano*. They organized **boycotts** against merchants who supported the slave trade and urged politicians to introduce laws banning the trade.

In 1785, the abolition movement found its leader. William Wilberforce was born in 1759 to a wealthy merchant family in the port city of Hull. He spent his teenage and early adult years in what he described as "utter idleness and dissipation." While a student at Cambridge—in between gambling, drinking, and late night parties—Wilberforce began a lifelong friendship with William Pitt the Younger, who would later be England's youngest prime minister. Pitt introduced Wilberforce to a new source of excitement: politics. Wilberforce was elected to the House of Commons in September, 1780, when he was only twenty-one.

In the fall of 1785, Wilberforce converted to Evangelical Christianity. His first thought was to leave Parliament and enter the church. John Newton, a former slave trader who had repented and become a leading Evangelical clergyman, convinced Wilberforce to stay in politics, where he could use his wealth and talent for the benefit of mankind.

Shortly after his conversion, Wilberforce became involved with the Clapham Sect and the Society for Effecting the Abolition of the Slave Trade. Wilberforce became a tireless sponsor of anti-slavery legislation. On May 12, 1789, he introduced twelve resolutions against the slave trade for consideration by Parliament. He spoke for more than three hours about the evil effects of the trade in Africa and the conditions of the infamous Middle Passage. Many newspapers at the time considered it the most eloquent speech ever given in the House of Commons, but the resolutions did not come to a vote. Instead the issue was postponed for review.

Two years of parliamentary hearings on the slave trade produced 1,700 pages of eyewitness accounts

British politician William Wilberforce (1759–1833) led the movement to pass legislation abolishing the British slave trade.

and other testimony before the House of Commons. Finally, the bill came to a vote in April 1791. The timing was bad. News arrived that a violent slave revolt had broken out on the British island of Dominica in the Caribbean. The pro-slavery advocates blamed the revolt on the abolitionists and argued that ending the slave trade would damage the British economy, which was already suffering from the war with France. Many members of Parliament opposed a bill they feared would encourage more slave revolts. The motion was defeated.

In response to the bill's failure, abolitionist forces sought to broaden their base of popular support with a flood of books, pamphlets, and public speeches denouncing the sale of human beings. They focused on winning over ministers, who then preached to their congregations about the evils of the slave trade. When Wilberforce proposed a new bill for abolishing the slave trade in 1792, it was supported by petitions signed by hundreds of thousands of British subjects. The debate lasted all night. To the disappointment of Wilberforce and his supporters, the House of Commons passed a compromise measure that called for the gradual abolition of slavery. The bill was subsequently killed in the House of Lords.

For the next fifteen years, Wilberforce proposed legislation to abolish the slave trade every year. Every year, Parliament voted it down. Finally, on February 23, 1807, Parliament passed a law abolishing the slave trade in British territories and making it illegal to carry slaves in British ships. The bill went into effect on May 1. Slavers who left British ports on or before that date could legally transport slaves to the Americas until March 1, 1808. The law did not free existing slaves in either Britain or its colonies.

Making the Ban Reality

The practical impact of British and American laws that abolished the slave trade was small at first. In fact, the scale of the trade increased. Brazil replaced Britain as the most important slave-trading nation. Other

The Slave Trade and the American Constitution

American colonists had already explored the possibility of abolishing the slave trade before the American Revolution. They did so not because it was wrong but because it was expensive and potentially dangerous. After a slave revolt that led to the death of sixty people in 1739, South Carolina attempted to stop the slave trade on the grounds that slaves newly imported from Africa brought with them the threat of revolt. Twice, in 1739 and 1760, South Carolina suspended the trade entirely. Twice, in 1751 and 1764, the colony imposed high taxes on African-born slaves to discourage the trade. Shortly before the revolution, Virginia also imposed prohibitively high taxes to discourage the trade. Many believed the slave trade diverted much-needed money from the colony. The British government overturned the colonial law each time because the trade was important to Britain's economy.

During the revolution, all thirteen colonies banned the slave trade as part of the boycott on British goods. When the Constitutional Convention met in Philadelphia in 1787, Georgia was the only state that had lifted the ban. Those who opposed the slave trade on moral grounds hoped the new constitution would ban the trade outright. States that were dependent on plantation slave labor fought to keep the right to import more slaves. In the end, the delegates compromised. Article 1, section 9 of the Constitution prevented the government from abolishing the slave trade prior to 1808.

On March 3, 1807, Thomas Jefferson signed into a law a bill making it illegal to import slaves into the United States after January 1, 1808. This was first date the Constitution allowed such an act to take effect.

European companies continued to trade in slaves, often with money from British investors. British slave traders continued to sail throughout the nineteenth century, sometimes registering their ships with foreign countries. At first, Britain used diplomatic measures to pressure other governments to outlaw the trade as well. For instance, at the Congress of Vienna in 1815, at the end of the Napoleonic Wars, Britain convinced France and the Netherlands to abolish the trade.

Soon, however, Britain resorted to force. Beginning in 1819, the British Navy attempted to enforce the ban by patrolling the African coastline and treating all slave ships as pirates. France and the United States reluctantly joined the effort. At least 160,000 slaves were rescued. Those who were not saved often suffered worse conditions in their voyage across the Atlantic than had previously existed in the Middle Passage. Since convicted slavers were executed for piracy, slavers sometimes threw their captives into the ocean when the authorities pursued them.

Despite the dangers of running the naval blockade, the slave trade continued through the 1860s. Scarcity meant higher prices for the shipments of slaves that reached the Americas. Slaves ships continued to openly smuggle slaves into the United States until shortly before the beginning of the Civil War. The last known slave shipment arrived in Cuba in 1864.

From Abolishing the Slave Trade to Abolishing Slavery

Wilberforce and his colleagues saw the Slave Trade Abolition Act of 1807 as only the first step in a campaign to abolish slavery altogether. In 1823, they

The British Navy patrolled the African coast looking for illegal slave traders. Captured slave traders were treated as pirates.

founded the Anti-Slavery Society, with the goal of abolishing slavery throughout the British Empire.

After serving in the House of Commons for forty-five years, Wilberforce retired in 1825. He turned over leadership of the abolitionist party in Parliament to Sir Thomas Fowell Buxton. Wilberforce was on his deathbed when the Abolition of Slavery Act was finally passed in July 1833. He died three days later. British slave owners received compensation for up to 40 percent of the estimated market value of their slaves. Slaves received only their freedom.

The fact that the most powerful nation in the world had freed its slaves raised the hope of abolitionists

This 1861 cartoon, published in a London paper with an offensive caption, shows that racist attitudes toward Africans continued after the slave trade ended there.

around the world. Millions of slaves remained in bondage. In 1833, there were more than 1.5 million slaves in Brazil, roughly 400,000 slaves in Cuba, and more than two million in the United States.

The British colonies in the Caribbean had once been the place where American slaves who caused trouble were banished: a fate to be feared. Now it was seen as a possible refuge. In 1841, 135 slaves who were in transit from Richmond to New Orleans on an American ship, the *Creole,* revolted. They hijacked the ship and forced it to sail to Nassau, which was the nearest British port. Once there, they demanded and gained their freedom, despite furious protests from the American consul.

Over the course of the nineteenth century, more countries outlawed slavery at home and in their colonies. One by one, the newly independent nations of Spanish America freed their slaves from the 1820s to the 1850s. The Thirteenth Amendment ended slavery in the United States in 1865 (the Emancipation Proclamation, which Abraham Lincoln issued in 1863, only freed slaves in the Confederate states). Portugal became the last European country to abolish slavery in 1869. In 1888, the last slaves in the Americas became free when Brazil abolished slavery. The transatlantic slave trade had come to an end.

Glossary

abolitionist A person who wants to abolish an institution or practice. Historically the term referred specifically to someone who wanted to abolish the slave trade.

asiento A license sold by the Spanish government that gave the purchaser permission to sell slaves in the Spanish colonies in Latin America and the Caribbean.

boycott A refusal to buy certain goods or participate in certain activities as as form of protest.

camel caravan A group of people, usually merchants or religious pilgrims, who travel together across a desert in Asia or North Africa using camels for transportation.

caravel A small, maneuverable sailing ship introduced by the Portuguese in the fifteenth century.

chandler A merchant who deals in supplies for ships and boats.

charter In the context of a corporation, a charter is given by the state that affords the company specific rights and privileges—usually a monopoly on trade in a certain region or for a specific item.

coffle A line of slaves connected by ropes or chains. Slaves were linked in a coffle to make it easier to march them across long distance.

dhow A sailing ship with triangular, or lateen, sails developed in the Red Sea and Indian Ocean.

the Enlightenment An eighteenth-century philosophical and scientific movement that shared a core set of values that included the power of reason and skepticism about existing social and political institutions.

eunuch A man whose testes have been removed, traditionally employed as a harem guard or government official in some cultures.

Evangelical Referring to a Christian sect or group that stresses the authority of the Bible. In nineteenth-century Britain, evangelical groups stood outside the established Church of England and were often associated with reform movements.

factories A historical term for trading posts used by merchants as warehouses, offices, and housing in a foreign country. This term was derived from the word "factor," which referred to someone who buys and sells as an agent for another person.

freedman A person was a slave but now has been given or purchased her freedom.

grassroots organizing The process of building a political or social justice movement using ordinary people, often outside of existing organizations.

gum arabic The dried gum of the acacia tress, which was used to make inks, dyes and medicine. Gum arabic is still used as a stabilizing ingredient in the food, printing, and textile industries.

hajj The pilgrimage to Mecca that every Muslim is required to make once in his lifetime.

indentured servants Workers who agreed to work for an employer for a specified period of time in order to work off the cost of their journey to the Americas.

indigo A plant used to make a blue dye used to color fabrics.

joint-stock company A variation on the chartered company in which capital was provided by shareholders who participated in the profits from the venture. Individual stockholders were not responsible for the company's actions.

lateen Triangular sails hung at a 45-degree angle to the mast. Used on both dhows and caravels, lateen sails could take the wind from either direction, which allowed a ship to tack into the wind.

maroon A runaway slave, from the Spanish *cimarrón,* meaning savage.

Middle Passage The transatlantic voyage of slaves from Africa to the Americas.

monopoly The exclusive right to sell a commodity or do business in a region. Having no competitor in a business or marketplace.

oases Fertile spots in a desert.

pilgrimage A journey of moral or religious significance.

privateer A private ship owner with a government license, called a letter of marque, giving him permission to attack foreign ships in time of war.

shallow draft Used to describe a ship or boat in which the bottom of the hull is not far below the waterline.

sub-Saharan The region of Africa south of the Sahara Desert.

topography The geographical features of a region.

Bibliography

Bailey, Anne C. *African Voices of the Atlantic Slave Trade*. Boston: Beacon, 2006.

Bellegamba, Alice, Sandra E. Greene and Martin A Klein, eds. *African Voices on Slavery and the Slave Trade*. New York: Cambridge University Press, 2013.

Benjamin, Thomas. *The Atlantic World: Europeans, Africans, Indians and Their Shared History, 1400–1900*. New York: Cambridge University Press, 2009.

Black, Jeremy. *The Atlantic Slave Trade in World History*. New York: Routledge, 2015.

Bovill, E. E. *The Golden Trade of the Moors*. Oxford, UK: Oxford University Press, 1968.

Burnside, Madeline and Rosemarie Robotham. *Spirits of the Passage: The Transatlantic Slave Trade in the Seventeenth Century*. New York: Simon and Schuster Editions, 1997.

Coughty, Jay. *The Notorious Triangle: Rhode Island and the African Slave Trade, 1700–1807*. Philadelphia: Temple University Press, 1998.

Crosby, Alfred. *The Columbian Exchange: Biological and Cultural Consequences of 1492*. Westport, CT: Greenwood Publishing Co., 1972.

Curtin, Philip D. *The Atlantic Slave Trade: A Census*. Madison, WI: University of Wisconsin Press, 1969.

Davidson, Basil. *The African Slave Trade*. Boston: Little, Brown and Company, 1980.

Davis, Ralph. *The Rise of the Atlantic Economies*. Ithaca, New York: Cornell University Press, 1973.

Eltis, David and David Richardson. *Atlas of the Transatlantic Slave Trade*. New Haven, CT: Yale University Press, 2010.

Hochschild, Adam. *Bury the Chains: Prophets and Rebels in the Fight to Free an Empire's Slaves*. Boston: Houghton Mifflin, 2005.

Howard, Thomas, ed. *Black Voyage: Eyewitness Accounts of the Atlantic Slave Trade*. Boston: Little, Brown and Company, 1971.

Meredith, Martin. *The Fortunes of Africa: A 5000-Year History of Wealth, Greed and Endeavor*. New York: Public Affairs, 2014.

Parker, Matthew. *The Sugar Barons: Family, Corruption, Empire and War in the West Indies*. New York: Walker and Company, 2011.

Russell, Peter. *Prince Henry "the Navigator": A Life*. New Haven, CT: Yale Nota Bene, 2001.

St. Clair, William. *The Door of No Return: The History of Cape Coast Castle and the Atlantic Slave Trade*. New York: Bluebridge, 2007.

Thomas, Hugh. *The Slave Trade. The Story of the Atlantic Slave Trade, 1440–1870*. New York: Simon and Schuster, 1997.

Thornton, John. *Africa and Africans in the Making of the Atlantic World, 1400–1800*. 2nd Edition. Cambridge, UK: Cambridge University Press, 1998.

Tibbles, Anthony, ed. *Transatlantic Slavery: Against Human Dignity*. London, UK: National Museums and Galleries on Merseyside, 1994.

Tomkins, Stephen. *William Wilberforce: A Biography*. Grand Rapids, MI: William B. Eerdmans Pub. Co., 2007.

Walvin, James. *Britain's Slave Empire*. Charleston, SC: Tempus Publishing, 2000.

———. *A Short History of Slavery*. New York: Penguin Books, 2007.

———. *The Trader, The Owner, The Slave: Parallel Lives in the Age of Slavery*. London: Jonathan Cape, 2007.

Further Information

Websites

The Abolition of Slavery Project
http://abolition.e2bn.org/
This site deals with the British abolition movement as the
first mass social movement and considers slave resistance
movements as well as the abolition campaign.

The Abolition of the Slave Trade
http://abolition.nypl.org/
The Schomburg Center for Research in Black Culture at
the New York Public Library hosts this useful collection
of essays, maps, timelines and images related to the slave
trade in the United States and its abolition.

The African Holocaust
http://www.africanholocaust.net/
An Afro-centric site dedicated to the study of African
history, the African Holocaust has a strong emphasis on the
African slave trade and its long-term consequences.

**The Atlantic Slave Trade and Slave Life in the Americas:
A Visual Record**
http://slaveryimages.org/
This large collection of digitized images related to the
Atlantic slave trade and slavery in North America was
collected by Jerome S. Handler and Michael L. Tuite, Jr.

Transatlantic Slave Trade Database
http://slavevoyages.org/
Explore an interactive database with information on 36,000 slave voyages.

Books

Curtin, Philip D. *Africa Remembered: Narratives by West Africans from the Era of the Slave Trade.* Madison, WI: University of Wisconsin Press, 1967.

Equiano, Olaudah. *Equiano's Travels: The Interesting Narrative of the Life of Olaudah Equiano or Gustavus Vassa, the African.* Portsmouth, NH: Heineman, 1996.

Newton, John. *The Journal of a Slave Trader (John Newton) 1750–1754.* London, UK: The Epworth Press, 1962.

Owen, Nicholas. *Journal of a Slave-Dealer.* London, UK: George Routledge and Sons, LTD., 1930.

Film and Video

"Africans in America"
http://www.pbs.org/wgbh/aia/home.html
This six-hour PBS series (with a related website) chronicles the history of slavery in the United States, from the start of the Atlantic slave trade in the sixteenth century through the end of the American civil War in 1865. The first episode, "The Terrible Transformation," focuses on the development of the slave trade.

"Amazing Grace"
http://www.amazinggracemovie.com
A biographical film of the life of William Wilberforce, directed by Michael Apted.

Index

Page numbers in **boldface** are illustrations. Entries in **boldface** are glossary terms.

About the Author

Pamela D. Toler is a freelance writer with a PhD in history and a lifelong fascination with the times and places where two cultures touch and change each other. Her work has appeared in *Aramco World, Calliope, History Channel Magazine, MHQ: The Quarterly Journal of Military History*, and *Victorian Home*. She is the author of a biography of Matt Damon, the *Everything Guide to Understanding Socialism, Mankind: the Story of All of Us*, companion volume to the History Channel series of the same name, and, most recently, *Heroines of Mercy Street: The Real Nurses of the Civil War*, a non-fiction companion to the PBS historical drama *Mercy Street*.

She currently lives in Chicago, where she is writing a history of women warriors. You can find her at her website, www.pameladtoler.com.